H. K Woods

KIDNAPPED

Kidnapped!

Eunice Diment's story

Exeter
The Paternoster Press

ISBN: 0 85364 199 4

Photograph on back cover:
Syndication International Ltd

AUSTRALIA
Emu Book Agencies Pty., Ltd.,
63 Berry Street, Granville, N.S.W., 2142

SOUTH AFRICA
Oxford University Press
P.O. Box 1141, Oxford House,
11, Buitencingle Street, Cape Town

Typeset by Input Typesetting Ltd, London and printed in Great Britain by Butler and Tanner for The Paternoster Press Ltd, Paternoster House, 3 Mount Radford Crescent, Exeter, Devon.

CONTENTS

Zamboanga and Basilan Island

The Philippines

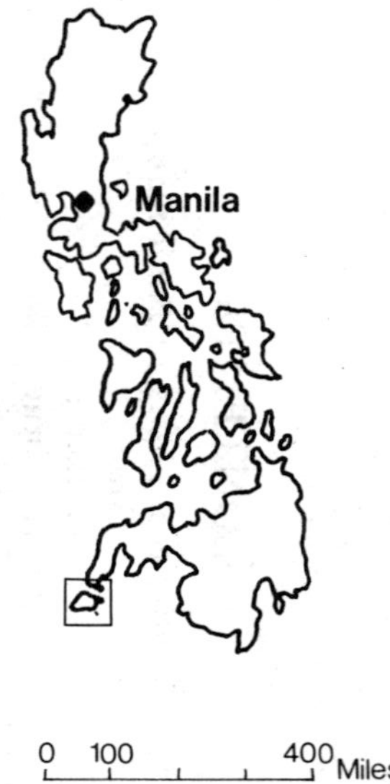

PREFACE

In 1971, Eunice Diment, a former tax-inspector and member of Preston Chapel, Yeovil, Somerset, joined Wycliffe Bible Translators and the Summer Institute of Linguistics (SIL) under whose auspices its work overseas is carried on. This consists principally in the study of unwritten languages, the translation of the Scriptures into these languages, and literacy work. Eunice believed that God was calling her to do Bible translation for a minority group in the Philippines, one of the twenty countries in which Wycliffe was then working.

En route to the Philippines, Eunice attended a special training course in Mexico designed to prepare new members to live in isolated and pioneer situations. This accomplished, she crossed the Pacific to arrive in Manila, where SIL's Philippines Branch has its headquarters, in July 1972. After spending nine months learning the national language, Tagalog, Eunice helped with the typing and finance work at a secondary headquarters at Nasuli, which serves SIL members working in the southern part of the Philippines.

By March 1974 Eunice, together with an American colleague, Jo Ann Gault, felt that God was leading them to work among the Bangingi Samal people, a Muslim group, who live along the coasts of southern Mindanao and on the islands of the Sulu Sea. At first they lived in cosmopolitan Zamboanga City, at the southern end of Mindanao, where there is a small community of Bangingi people. From Zamboanga they visited some of the offshore islands which were more distinctly Bangingi to find a better place for getting to know the people and their language. At the beginning of March 1975 they moved to Panigayan on a little island called Malamawi, which lies close to the larger island of Basilan, itself a two-hour boat ride from Zamboanga.

Until they could arrange for their own house to be built, Eunice and Jo Ann were guests of a Bangingi family of three generations. An unmarried son, Sulaiman, a respected local leader, was in charge of the house-building project. Soon Jo Ann and Eunice became part of the family and were "adopted" as daughters of the household.

Late in 1975 they moved into their own home, built of local materials and raised on stilts over the water. By the beginning of 1976 Eunice was able to write home in a prayer letter:

> "These are exciting days for me in Panigayan as I work on translating the Old Testament story of Joseph. It is such a joy to have the privilege and responsibility of putting God's Word into the Bangangi Samal language for the first time."

On February 28, three weeks after Eunice's thirty-seventh birthday and four months before her first furlough, the news flashed round the world that she had been kidnapped.

Saturday, February 28

The first I knew there was anything wrong that Saturday morning was consternation in the back of the boat. I thought another boat had run into us. Sometimes that happens with these pumpboats – outrigger canoes powered by inboard motors. "It's just an accident," I said to myself. Then I saw the man in the front of the boat standing there with a pistol and I realised it wasn't an accident.

"Oh God! We're being held up! Are they going to rob us, or kill us, or both? Help, Lord!" He was a young man with wild-looking eyes and a woollen balaclava on his head. I was sure the pistol was loaded – "Oh please Lord, don't let anybody be killed."

I could hear Sulaiman, my language-helper and a member of our adopted Bangingi family, trying to reason with the fellow in Bangingi and I heard the word *"pote"* mentioned. I knew what it meant. "*White* – they're talking about me. I'm the only white person in this boat. I'm going to be kidnapped. Oh God!"

Nobody said anything to me. Finally the members of my adopted family in the boat said, "You'd better go with them." "Do I have to go?" I asked. They said, "Yes, you go with them and Sulaiman will go with you." It occurred to me that anything I took with me was likely to be stolen. My bag and its contents must stay behind – tape recorder, paper and pens, handbag containing money and documents. But I took my umbrella, useful in rain or sunshine.

I transferred to the boat and Sulaiman came with me. I don't suppose I'll ever forget the sight of my friends sitting in their pumpboat, while we sped off, for somewhere, I knew not where.

At the time I saw only the one boat. Later on a second one with more armed men in it caught up with us. I heard some shooting. "Oh no! Are they going to come and get me from this lot?" But I suppose they were firing their guns in celebration. It was frightening, especially when the fellow right behind me shot off his big gun. I instinctively turned round and said to him in Bangingi "Don't!" He didn't do it again!

It was an uncomfortable boat-ride, as I tried to keep my balance, sitting on an empty five-gallon water container. The sea was quite heavy and we got wet, but my captors kindly gave me an old plastic jacket to shield me a bit from the spray. After an hour and a half we arrived at our destination and were told to get out of the boat. It was 11.0 a.m. by my watch. The sea was quite deep and Sulaiman had to help me wade ashore. We were hustled along through some mangrove swamps – these scrubby trees grow around most of the islands of that area – until we reached a sandy beach. They told us to go inside the cover of the undergrowth and small trees that bordered the beach, so that we wouldn't be seen by passers-by.

We sat down on some old logs and surveyed our situation. "Do you think you could stay alive, Ma'am, in this place?" one of my captors asked. "How polite he is," I thought, "calling me 'Ma'am'." I looked around me . . . "Yes, I think so, if it isn't for long," I replied. My mind went back a few years to the Jungle Camp training I had attended in Mexico in early 1972. They had taught us how to survive in the jungle; how to build a shelter, what to look for to eat, how to make a good fire to ward off wild animals. This wasn't even jungle – no wild animals here. I should be able to survive.

We didn't have to look for our own food: before long our captors brought us Coca-Cola drinks and bread rolls that they had bought at a little shop not too far away. This was repeated later in the afternoon. Meanwhile, various people came to look at us; others came and talked.

Everyone was obviously gathering and our captors told us that they were waiting for the arrival of the leaders of the Moro National Liberation Front (MNLF) who would say what was to happen to us.

I felt encouraged because I could speak their language, Bangingi, and I could understand all that was going on. Everybody seemed quite sympathetic and I thought, "It must all be a mistake. They'll probably realise they have the wrong person and perhaps they will send us home later on." When their leaders arrived, however, I was soon discouraged. They were different, with cold, steely eyes. One introduced himself as "Commander J–", then introduced the other man and said "This is Commander S–, the head of our Liquidation Squad." Commander J– just gazed at me and I felt very frightened. "Oh God, what's going to happen now?" Then they questioned us. "Didn't you know there's a war going on here?" That question was to come up many times in the next few weeks. I explained that we were aware of the unrest in the whole Sulu area and of sporadic fighting between members of the MNLF and Government soldiers, but that we had considered our area to be fairly peaceful at present. They also asked our purpose in being there. They were sure Sulaiman was some kind of government agent and that was why he had come with me. At that moment I realised that Sulaiman had taken a great risk in volunteering to come with me. Now he might be in more danger than I was. I wished he hadn't come. I tried to convince my captors that he was just like a brother, but they remained suspicious.

We were there all day . . . answering questions, praying, thinking. I went over the events of the day in my mind. It was unbelievable that such a routine boat–journey should have ended up like this. My co-worker Jo Ann Gault and I had made the journey dozens of times before. From our home in the little Muslim community of Panigayan it took only 15 minutes to reach the town of Isabela on the larger island of Basilan. A Bangingi friend in Isabela had been expecting me that morning to finish recording the story of Joseph. I had started to translate this Old Testament story and she was telling me the story in her own words, in Bangingi. She must have heard by now what had happened to me. Sulaiman had helped me with the translation of the story, and now we were both living through a similar experience, carried away captive. How strange it all was.

I wondered where Jo Ann was now – what had she done when she heard the news? I hoped that she had been able to contact our Centre at Nasuli in Mindanao by means of our two-way radio. Perhaps our director there, Seymour Ashley, had already left for Zamboanga City and would be with Jo Ann soon. I was glad that Jo Ann had decided to stay at home today. She would be a great help at the other end. We usually went everywhere together but today our family were taking their boat and would wait for me so that I could come home with them. We were quite a boat-load too – 13 of us, including three small children. They must have all been terribly shocked, but at least no one had been hurt.

Now it was getting dusk. We were allowed to come out of cover and sit by the edge of the water. The tide was coming in. As I watched it lapping on the shore I sudden-

Saturday, February 28

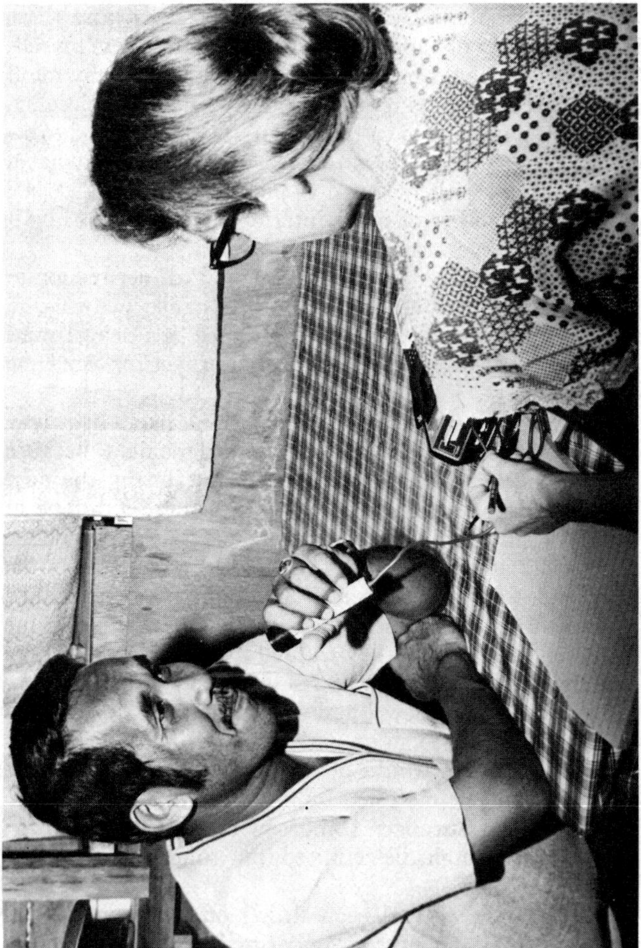

ly wondered if there were any pretty shells on this beach. One of my hobbies was collecting sea shells, and these were especially precious to me if I had found them myself. Surely there would be some here! It would take my mind off my circumstances if I were to look – but only close by, for I dare not move in case the men think I'm trying to escape. "Yes, there's one within easy reach!" And what a pretty one – as I bent down to pick it up I could see the glint of its mother-of-pearl interior. It was small but it would be a lovely souvenir.

Immediately after sunset Sulaiman asked permission to pray. They allowed him to go a little distance away and to borrow a piece of their polythene to use as a prayer-mat. So he prayed the appropriate Muslim prayer for that time of day.

After it got dark our captors took Sulaiman a little way off for "conversation". That was a hard moment, because his presence had been a comfort to me during the day. When he'd gone and I was left sitting there all alone in the dark surrounded by armed men, I felt frightened – defenceless and vulnerable. I realised I had to trust in the Lord and not in the presence of Sulaiman. It was good I realised it at that moment, because when Sulaiman came back, he told me that they wanted to take me somewhere else that night and he was going to be left behind. My heart sank, but I knew I had to put my trust in the Lord and just be ready to go on with Him, without any human companions. God would be with me. Sulaiman assured me I wouldn't be molested by my captors; and they gave me a similar assurance. Tomorrow or the following day, they said, we might be reunited, but somehow I thought we wouldn't be.

All the time we had been sitting on the beach, I was trying to recall Scripture, wondering how the Lord would comfort me. Psalm 23 came to mind. It is such a well-known Psalm, but now it took on new meaning for me. "God is with me, and He will look after me." Another verse that I felt very sure of at that time was Daniel 3:17: ". . . our God . . . is able to deliver us . . . and He will deliver us . . ." I held on to this throughout the day and that night as we set off again by boat for our next destination.

It was dark except for the light from their torches. After a lot of signals . . . calling and flashing . . . we left. As we went along Commander J– talked to me about our situation and said he might ask for 1 million pesos in ransom. I was staggered – that's about £77,000. He went on to say that if the ransom was not paid, Sulaiman would be killed. Again I wished that Sulaiman hadn't come with me. He really was in danger. As we went a little further, Commander J– asked me if I could see the lights of the fishermen out at sea. I could see them, so he asked me to close my eyes. Then after a little while he said, "Perhaps it would be better if you put that *tadjung* over your head." I had been lent one of these tubular skirts earlier in the day, to use as a covering when I had to go to the toilet in the bushes. Now I was wearing it over my shoulders for warmth. As instructed, I put it over my head to make sure I wouldn't see where we were going. I don't know where we went, but then I didn't really know where we were, except that it must be on the north-east corner of Basilan island. We were in the boat for about 50 minutes, finally wading to another shore at 8.30 p.m. It is possible that we actually went round in circles and ended up not far from our starting point and that is perhaps why I was not allowed to see where we went.

On the beach I sat down on a big piece of driftwood shaped like an armchair; it was nice and comfortable. My captors brought me something to eat – a plate of cold rice, a boiled fish-head and some shark, cooked in a sauce. It wasn't very appetising and I wasn't very hungry, but I ate a little. Commander J– volunteered to help me eat it. Then he said, "Let's go now."

We set off walking along the narrow trail. It was mostly uphill, and muddy in places. We walked in single file, Commander J– in the lead and I immediately behind him. I was thankful to be given a torch to hold and felt sorry for the men behind me who had to manage in the dark, carrying their guns and a sack of rice. But they seemed to be used to it.

I didn't know what sort of place I was being taken to, but prayed all the way there that it would be a house and that women would be there. It was a great relief when we got there, after 40 minutes of walking, to find women opening the door and saying, "Come up." It was a typical Muslim house, built on stilts and reached by a staircase made of bamboo poles which led up to a small verandah.

More food was prepared, but I didn't want anything else to eat so I went to bed in a small room which I shared with the women of the household. I still had on all my damp clothes from wading but I was lent a thin blanket, a pillow and a mat. This was not the first time I had slept on the floor, and I knew that the mat, woven from dried leaves, would help keep out the draught coming up through the split bamboo floor. As I lay in the darkness two things came into my mind. One was: "Sufficient unto the day is the evil thereof"[1] – only half a verse but I said "Amen" to that. The other was the experience of my SIL colleagues, John and Carolyn Miller, during their eight months of captivity in Vietnam. I was very grateful to God that I had been at our Nasuli Centre in Mindanao when the Millers arrived there en route to the USA in October 1975 and I had heard their report. They testified to

[1] Matthew 6:34

the ways in which the Lord had helped them in their situation, which had been a lot worse than mine. It encouraged me and sustained me during those days to think of them. I thought of the words which had become a sort of joke for the Millers and their other missionary companions, "Prepare for one more night". So I prepared for my first night. I didn't go to sleep but went through the events of the day in my mind to make sure I wouldn't forget anything.

Sunday, February 29

I sat in my little room, which was really the women's bedroom and changing-room. It was a sort of extension of the house with walls made from the woven leaves of the nipa palm tree. The house itself was small, with a thatch roof and wooden walls. There was no furniture, but clothes were stored in large wooden boxes and suitcases. My room had no window but there was a gap in the nipa in one of the corners, and people going across the plank "bridge" between the verandah and the kitchen could look in at me. A doorway led out into the main room.

The women had got up early and made a variety of Muslim delicacies for breakfast, which was brought to me in my room on a tray – the typical Muslim way of serving a guest. Everyone else ate in the kitchen. I was offered the use of a communal toothbrush and toothpaste, and borrowed a comb from the women. Then I felt a bit better, but wondered how long it would be before I could get hold of a change of clothes. The ones I was wearing –

slacks and a blouse – were dry now, but needed washing. Perhaps the women would lend me some of their clothes . . .

For the first part of the morning I sat and thought and prayed. Around 10.0 a.m. I was told, "Now you will write a letter". Instructions were given in Bangingi as to whom I should write to and what the contents should be. I was left to decide on the format of the letter myself. I wrote the first letter to Dan Weaver, Director of SIL in the Philippines, then one to the British Embassy and one to my co-worker, Jo Ann. Now I knew the amount of the ransom demand: it was 200,000 pesos (about £15,000) not one million pesos as I had been told the previous evening. I was relieved about that. But when I had finished writing suddenly everything seemed to hit me. Up until that time it hadn't seemed real. Now I got a bit weepy and wondered what was going to happen to me.

The house where I stayed belonged to a Tausug family (members of another Muslim group whose home is in the Sulu area), and they grew coconuts, manioc (cassava), some vegetables and fruit on their land. Because they lived in an area frequented by the MNLF soldiers they were obliged to help them by providing food and shelter, and doing all they were asked to do. So my captors stayed in the house too. The family consisted of five sisters and their widowed father. Two of the girls were married and had husbands there. One of them had two children. Another of the girls was a widow – her husband had been killed by the MNLF soldiers for refusing to do as he was asked. The other two girls were unmarried. The family were very concerned about me and wanted to make sure I wasn't hungry or thirsty or worried. They did their best to encourage me along these lines and to bring all sorts of food and generally try to cheer me up. Some of them could speak Bangingi and some of them couldn't, so they either spoke to me in Tausug, which I didn't understand, or they just sat and looked at me.

Many other people came to look at me too. This was to be a daily occurrence. Some came to talk, others just sat and looked.

During the afternoon I had a pleasant surprise – a brown carrier-bag arrived containing some clothes and a few toilet articles. Now I didn't have to live indefinitely in what I had on! The letters had been taken over to Panigayan and the couriers had collected clothes for Sulaiman and for myself from our homes there. Sulaiman's sister had gone around and tried to find the things she thought I would need. There were my two long tubular skirts and the three Muslim-style blouses I wore all the time in Panigayan; several items of underwear; a cardigan, and the cotton slacks that matched the blouse I was wearing. The two latter items would be especially good to wear at night. Then there was my towel and face-cloth, soap, toothbrush and paste, hair brush, talcum powder, toilet paper, rubbing alcohol (good for wounds, mosquito-bites, etc.), and headache pills . . . Thank you, Lord. Days later when I saw what was obviously my deodorant being used by one of my captors I realised that there must have been other items in that bag, too.

The couriers reported that my adopted Bangingi mother was crying all the time and wasn't eating anything, and that my older sister was also crying. Later I was to learn that my "mother" fainted from worry and lack of food, and my elderly "uncle" suffered a stroke and was hospitalised for several days. Such was the grief of my adopted family as they wondered what fate awaited Sulaiman and me. And as for us, we were clearly going to be kept in different places, for Sulaiman didn't arrive that day.

In the late afternoon I was allowed out on to the verandah. It was nice to feel the fresh air and to see the view – the sea below and an island in the distance. We were surrounded by trees, mostly coconut palms or bananas, and there were no other houses in sight. Best of all, there was a bench along one side of the verandah and this was a welcome change from sitting on the floor. I was still on the verandah when my evening meal was brought to me on a tray. I would have to eat it with everyone watching me. Seeing my hesitation, Commander J– came over. "It's not poisoned. To prove it, I'll eat some too." Poison . . . the idea had never crossed my mind! He sat down and ate with me.

In the evening I sat with the household and they thought we should be cheerful and do some singing. One of the girls sang some of the Muslim songs and then they told me it was my turn. I was glad of this opportunity to show them that you could sing in praise of the Lord. They thought it was laughing at God to sing about Him, but seemed to change their minds when they heard the songs. I sang two songs, "What a friend we have in Jesus" and "How good is the God we adore". The latter is a very precious one to me. I had chosen it for my valedictory service held at Preston Chapel, Yeovil, before leaving England in January 1972. It seemed to sum up my sentiments then, and it did so now:–

How good is the God we adore,
  Our faithful, unchangeable Friend!
His love is as great as His power,
  And knows neither measure nor end!

'Tis Jesus the First and the Last,
  Whose Spirit shall guide us safe home;
We'll praise Him for all that is past,
  We'll trust Him for all that's to come.

I needed assurance of His love and power at that moment,

and I certainly needed to trust Him for the uncertain days ahead.

Monday, March 1

After breakfast, water was brought to the house and I was able to have a bath and change my clothes. It was a wonderful feeling. Then I had another interview with Commander J–. Both he and Commander S– were living in the house with their small company of men, varying from five to twelve in number. I asked why I had been kidnapped, and was told that they didn't have anything against us, Jo Ann or me, or anything against SIL. The main reason for my kidnapping was to give their cause publicity and make other countries aware that there was a revolution going on in the Philippines. As we were talking, an Imam, a religious leader from one of the local mosques, came and sat in the doorway. When I asked "Where is Sulaiman? Is he living in a house?", because I wondered if he was being kept somewhere on the beach, the Imam said "He's in my house in Lamitan I; he's all right." I was in an area called Lamitan II. Both of these are large rural areas, surrounding the town of Lamitan, and divided for administrative purposes. I was relieved to know that Sulaiman was being well treated so far.

Later on a plane flew over and dropped some letters. Everyone was very excited, saying, "That's the reply to your letters!" But it turned out to be information about the peace talks which were to be held shortly in the area between representatives of both the government and the

MNLF. As I found out later, the letters I had written hadn't yet been delivered.

A number of visitors came during the day – mostly MNLF soldiers. There was a lot of teasing from the commanders and the men. They liked the fact that I wore Muslim clothes and could speak their language. It would be very nice, they said, for me to have a Bangingi husband and they suggested that I should marry Commander J–. I assured them that I had no intention of marrying anybody there. It occurred to me that perhaps I should try to tone down my Bangingi image a bit. I didn't want to appear too desirable as a wife. So I abandoned my intention to ask if I could help the women with the food preparation, and didn't reveal the fact that I knew how to clean rice. And I stopped taking much interest in the children, since this provoked unwelcome remarks too. The days seemed long with nothing to do – no work, nothing to read, nothing to write . . . It was boring.

Later that evening there was more teasing when Commander J– was sick with a headache. The other men said to me, "There, you see? Because you don't like him, he's sick!" Commander J– himself asked me if I had any medicine for headaches, and I got out the ones that Sulaiman's sister had sent. He didn't recognize them, since they weren't "aspirin", and was reluctant to take them. "They're not poison, are they?" "No," I replied. "They're good."

During the day, a verse that often came to mind was one that Dick Pittman, the Director of Asian Studies for SIL International, had shared during a recent visit. "The Lord on high is mightier than the noise of many waters, yea, than the mighty waves of the sea." [1] Dick had testified how this verse had encouraged him in a difficult

[1] Psalm 93:4

situation in another country, and he had composed a tune to go with it and taught it to us. Now I was singing it. It was a great strength to remember that no matter how noisy all the waves seemed to sound, God was greater than all these things. I held on to that.

In conversation with some of the men, I discovered that the kidnappers had been definitely looking for Jo Ann and me. I don't know if they knew we were going to be out on the water that day; they didn't imply that, but they asked me where we had come from a couple of months before, because we hadn't been on Panigayan for a while. It was a shock to realise that my kidnapping wasn't a fluke; we were their target. The ransom was going to be 500,000 pesos (about £38,500) for the two of us. When they got only me, there was a delay while they had to send over to Zamboanga del Sur for fresh instructions. They often mentioned Jo Ann though, and I wondered if they would try and get her too. I hoped she would be careful if she was still in the Panigayan area. If only I could warn her . . .

During the three weeks of Eunice's captivity, Dan Weaver, Philippines Branch Director, sent messages of encouragement via the two-way radio sets which most members of the Branch have in their locations. The first message was sent on March 1:

It has been reported by the Philippine Constabulary and by Seymour that the general location of Eunice and her abductors is known. A delegation of authorities has already left for the site to initiate negotiations. It is not known who are members of the delegation but Seymour is not part of the delegation.

Tuesday, March 2

One member of the delegation offered to take a letter to Eunice. Seymour is sending a note, a Bible, a few medicines and a mosquito-net. We have been assured by the authorities that they are doing all they can to obtain Eunice's release. I recommend Psalm 46 for your encouragement. We have a great God. Do not be dismayed.

Tuesday, March 2

I had to write the letters again, because the originals had not been delivered. Everybody was afraid to handle them, so they had been brought back.

To Summer Institute of Linguistics
(Dan Weaver via Seymour Ashley)
DEAR DAN,

You know by now that I was kidnapped last Saturday from a pumpboat going to Isabela, and that Sulaiman from our Bangingi family voluntarily came with me. We are now being held in different places in Basilan interior, Sulaiman at Lamitan I and I at Lamitan II. We have both been well-treated so far.

I have been informed of the requirements for safe release as told to me by Commander S– of the MNLF, Zamboanga del Sur. These are as follows:–

1. Ransom money of P200,000, to be in *cash*, not cheques, and not to be fake money.
2. Two pairs of binoculars (or at least one) with 75 x 50 lenses. They say these can be bought in Manila.

3. These to be brought by pumpboat to a point 10 kilometres off the coast of Basilan, in the direction of Lamitan if starting from Isabela.
4. There must be no military intervention.
5. No more than *three* people to bring the money – being one member of SIL and two Bangingis from Panigayan. The military must *not* be involved in bringing the money.
6. On receipt of these demands they guarantee the safe return of Sulaiman and myself to Panigayan.
7. The money must be brought by next *Friday, 5th March* (original time limit, but now subject to extension).
8. If not, I will be taken immediately by speedboat to the interior of Zamboanga del Sur, and Sulaiman will be killed.

Dan, I don't know if my family has been told by now, but I would rather they don't know until after my safe release – unless of course the news is out in England. I leave that to you.

Thanks a lot for your help. I pray that this letter will reach you in time.

In His bonds,
EUNICE

While I was writing that letter, the first negotiator or go-between arrived – a woman. I did not know her, but she told me she was the sister-in-law of someone I knew, who was related to our Bangingi family. To my great delight she had brought a box of things sent by Jo Ann and Seymour Ashley, who was obviously now with Jo Ann in Isabela. There were a few more items of clothing, a mosquito-net, assorted medicines, reading-books in the Tausug language (prepared by Seymour and Lois Ashley who had spent many years living with the Tausug people), a small copy of the New Testament and Psalms and a short letter. I was encouraged by the letter which assured me of the prayers of many people, and also quoted Psalm 93:4. So once again I was reminded that "the Lord on high is *mightier* than the noise of many waters, yea, than the mighty waves of the sea". I knew that it was safe to trust such a God. And now I would be able to draw strength and encouragement from the Scriptures. How happy I was to have that little book!

Since I now had to rewrite my letter to Jo Ann, I enlarged it to include my thanks for the box, and I wrote:–

> Thanks a lot for the things you sent, especially the Word. It's good to have something to read at last. Sulaiman's sister also sent me some welcome items of clothing and toilet things.
>
> Try not to worry too much – I'm sorry you didn't receive the letters I wrote on Sunday, but here's a repeat of the one to SIL. Seymour will no doubt handle it as he's there with you. I know you're all praying for us both – Christians and Muslims. Isn't it something?
>
> The medicine is good to have, especially as the Commander is down with malaria today. I think I can still receive things so could you please send some notepaper and a ballpen, so that I can write. It's awful having nothing to do all day. Also a packet of Modess and accessories, and newspaper . . . I'll really need that soon. Thanks.
>
> We're well, but I'm not very hungry and can't eat all the food offered. Be careful, Jo Ann, as you travel around, use a *tadjung*.
>
> Oh, Jo Ann and Seymour . . . they told me after the other letters were written that the Government must not be informed about all this or both Sulaiman and I will be killed. If already informed (as I imagine) please

withdraw. May God help you to know what to do. It all seems unreal, but I guess it's happening. Ps. 23.

Love and prayers,

EUNICE

When the negotiator left she took my letters with her.

Another visitor had spent the previous night in the house where Sulaiman was being kept. He had gone there because he was worried by rumours he had heard, indicating that Sulaiman might be killed. He assured me, however, that Sulaiman was still all right, and I was relieved to know that.

After lunch, I went to sleep. As I had hardly been sleeping at all at night, I fell into a really deep sleep and so missed the arrival of another negotiator. I was woken up and asked to write a letter to the Philippine Constabulary chief in Zamboanga City, requesting some food. I must have been only half awake when I wrote the letter otherwise I wouldn't have asked for peanut butter, since I dislike it intensely! But they dictated the letter to me, in English, and this is what I wrote:–

DEAR COLONEL,

Kindly send us food supply for the daily sustainment of ours:–

1 sack good rice
20 packages American loaf bread
1 big tin Ovaltine
1 bottle Lady's Choice preserves
1 bottle Peanut Butter
10 kilos white sugar

EUNICE DIMENT

Note: Please send through the bearer of this note.

I found out later that this man was sent as a negotiator by the Colonel who was handling all the negotiations with my captors.

Tuesday, March 2

With a copy of the New Testament and Psalms I now had something to read. I started at Psalm 1 and read a number of Psalms each day. I had never realised before what the Psalmist went through. Many times he cries to the Lord for deliverance from affliction and I could identify myself with him. For example, Psalm 6 verses 2 and 3: "Have mercy upon me, O Lord; for I am weak: O Lord, heal me; for my bones are vexed. My soul is also sore vexed: but thou, O Lord, how long?" Well, my bones were sore from lying on the floor. My soul was vexed too. I could really identify with that and ask the Lord, "How long?" I'm glad I didn't know how long! I drew comfort from the fact that this was the experience of the Psalmist and I could know the victory that he had known through the Lord. I had great hope of deliverance in those early days, from reading the Psalms. The Psalmist had great assurance of deliverance; and I had that same assurance.

I gave the Tausug literature to the household, and it was interesting to see everyone's reactions to it. Some of my captors only glanced at it, but others spent hours poring over it. I knew that Seymour had sent it for their benefit so that they could see the kind of work our organisation was engaged in. Members of the family were interested in the books, too. One of the men taught his little boy the names of the pictures from the earliest preprimer. And one of the girls asked me to teach her how to read. I was glad of the extra reading material, too, and amused myself by seeing how much Tausug I could understand.

Commander J–'s sickness turned out to be malaria, so I gave him some of the medicine, Aralin, that had arrived in the box. I started to take it myself as a prophylactic, at the same time praying that the Lord would keep me from sickness. Before I left that house, four people had malarial attacks and there were many requests for medicine from these and other people who were sick.

It struck me as incongruous that my captors with their strange attire and headgear and their guns should put it all aside five times a day and pray the Muslim prayers. Quite a number of them were very faithful in praying. What a strange situation! I had mixed reactions to it. On the one hand it seemed to give a normalcy to my situation, since I was used to living with Muslims who pray regularly. The familiar sound of Arabic prayers lessened the strangeness of my daily life there. It also encouraged me to believe that my captors were at least outwardly practising Muslims and therefore less likely to molest me and so incur the anger of God. But on the other hand such devout praying seemed incompatible with their actions – such as kidnapping me and holding me captive.

Radio message from Dan Weaver, Branch Director, to all SIL members in the Philippines:

March 2

Government authorities are continuing negotiations with the kidnappers but no reports have been received. Seymour is maintaining constant contact with authorities in Isabela. The British Embassy is making contacts at highest levels in Manila. Various parties are doing everything possible.

Prayer should be made for Sulaiman as well as for Eunice. He is her landlord and Barangay secretary of Panigayan. Remember his family also. He voluntarily accompanied Eunice out of concern for her welfare.

Eunice was on her way to Isabela to record the story of Joseph on tape when abducted. Remember Genesis 50:20, and rejoice.

Wednesday, March 3

Early in the morning Commander J– walked into the room wearing my sandals which had been left outside on the verandah since I arrived. He asked if he could have them. "How will I be able to go home to Zamboanga City if I have no sandals?" I asked. "We'll buy you some rubber thongs," he replied. "Oh, I'd be ashamed to go home wearing rubber thongs," I said. "Well, if these sandals are precious to you," he responded, "keep them by your side." So I still had my sandals . . . and I kept them inside the room after that.

Some batteries were obtained for a portable radio which my captors said they had acquired from a Japanese lady who had been kidnapped about 6 months previously. The radio was left on all day in case there might be any news. Fortunately there was nothing. We never did hear over the radio anything that was connected with my kidnapping. I suppose we missed the initial announcement because of the lack of batteries.

Lots of people came to visit. It seemed there was always someone sitting and looking at me. They talked to each other about me, commenting on my ability to speak their language, and to eat their food. The tourists who had been kidnapped, they said, refused to eat anything but bread and would drink only Coca-cola. I felt for those tourists, and was very thankful to God that I had lived in our Bangingi family's home for five months, eating their food and learning their language and culture. That experience was standing me in good stead now.

Many of the visitors expressed sympathy for my plight, and asked "Aren't you longing for your mother?" I wished they wouldn't ask that. "Of course I am. I'm worried about her – she may be ill by now, wondering what is happening to me." It upset me to be reminded of my mother . . . and I was often near to tears. It was one of the hardest days of my captivity.

Once more I drew strength and comfort from reading and singing the Scriptures. I reached Psalm 22, which describes the Lord's sufferings as he was mocked by men. I felt in a similar position, but I remembered how much worse it was for Him. I also remembered His love, and His forgiveness and His longsuffering. I really prayed that I might have the same kind of attitude.

The Lord also brought a principle to my mind. Psalm 20: 7 reads "Some trust in chariots, some in horses: but we will remember the name of the Lord our God." Many times the Lord reminded me not to put my trust in anything or anybody, only in Him. In view of the different negotiators who came and went and the resulting disappointments, it was good to be reminded not to put my trust in any of these things.

In the afternoon most of the men went down to the shore, leaving Commander S– behind. Since there were so few people around I was invited to spend more time out on the verandah. The radio was still on and as a result the bird in a cage on the verandah began to sing. I enjoyed listening to him, and talking to him too. God had given me this little pleasure.

Soon Commander S– requested that we exchange watches. He had a nice big Seiko man's watch, automatic and with a calendar. I said, "Yours is much better than mine!" which wasn't automatic, and didn't have a calendar. But mine was an Omega and he no doubt wanted the prestige of having the "Americano's" watch. I didn't see how I could refuse, so the exchange was made.

When the other men returned they brought the food sent by the Colonel. I heard later that he had sent everything asked for, so it had obviously been divided between several households. We received part of a sack of rice, two loaves of sliced bread, about two-thirds of a tin of Ovaltine, and a jar of strawberry jam, half-full. I didn't see how much sugar there was. They must have taken note of my reaction to the peanut butter request, since none arrived at our house – though the food, of course, was eaten by everybody, not just by me.

Another letter was brought from Jo Ann and Seymour. Their letters were read by the two Commanders who knew English and I was asked to explain certain things – from the first letter, Psalm 93:4 "The Lord on high is mightier than the noise of many waters . . .". It was hard to explain in Bangingi, but I tried. This second letter confirmed that the letters written by me had now arrived, and encouraged me to read Psalms 62 and 116. As I read Psalm 62, verse 11 struck me, "Power belongeth unto God", and I added to myself, "*not* to my captors". That was another good principle that I found to be strengthening to remember day by day.

That night, as usual, I thought about the events of the past few days, going over them in my mind and trying to remember everything. I didn't have a pencil or pen yet so nothing had been written down. After several hours I finally realised that I was carrying all the burden of what had happened, and trying to find a solution to my predicament myself. Then the Lord brought to mind the verse, "Casting all your care upon him; for he careth for you." [1] "Of course! *God* will work out the solution to this. I can trust Him."

[1] 1 Peter 5:7

Radio Message from Dan Weaver, Branch Director:
March 3

We were informed by authorities in Zamboanga that a note was received by them allegedly from Eunice. Seymour and Jo Ann flew to Zamboanga this morning and verified Eunice's handwriting. Among other things, she asked for food and some is being sent. Seymour has been able to send a letter to Eunice assuring her of our prayers. I asked that Psalm 116 be included. We have been informed that Eunice is well.

Negotiations continue. The authority in charge, who successfully negotiated the safe release of a previous kidnappee, is hopeful for successful negotiations. Particularly remember authorities and persons responsible for negotiations.

Psalm 18 is our assurance for today, particularly verses 16 and 17: "Be strong and of good courage."

Thursday, March 4

Last night Commander J– and some of the men left to visit another island. The atmosphere seemed to relax a bit when he had gone and the women of the family were more friendly to me. Commander S–, who was left in charge of me, was friendly too. I was getting plenty of practice in speaking Bangingi, and found my fluency and accuracy increasing. Correctly-formed sentences seemed to come out without any effort. I must be picking up correct patterns just by hearing my captors talk day after day. Sometimes I wished I had my language notebook and pencil so that I could write down Bangingi utterances that would be useful in language-learning and analysis. I finally plucked up courage and asked if I could borrow a pen for this purpose. I did have some paper – an envelope that one of the letters from Jo Ann had been enclosed in, and the sheet of paper I had made notes on before writing my first letter to SIL. So I now wrote down some of the new Bangingi words and phrases I could remember having heard, and at the same time wrote brief diary entries for each day from Saturday onwards. Now the memory load wouldn't be so great and I wouldn't have to stay awake at night!

It was a very quiet, restful day for me. The Lord assured me from the Psalms that there was a set time for my deliverance. "My times are in thy hand: deliver me from the hand of my enemies . . ." [1]

The Tausug family continued their watchful care of me. The old man couldn't speak Bangingi, but he would come and stand in the doorway for a moment and look at me. Then he would report to his daughters if he felt that I was hungry, and tell them to start cooking. The girls were kept very busy preparing food for so many people. They made a variety of Muslim delicacies for breakfast, and twice a day we ate rice and fish. Since I ate first they always made sure that there was some fish for me, even it if was only the tinned variety. I was thankful to be offered plenty of food, but sometimes I didn't have much appetite, especially when there was a large audience. For their part they were probably fascinated to see a white woman eating rice and fish with her fingers. I was glad I had had plenty of practice at this in Panigayan, so could at least make a fairly good job of it.

[1] Psalm 31:15

As yet I hadn't had a good night's sleep, so I prayed about it that night and I slept really well. The Lord answered so many prayers about little things that I was encouraged to trust Him for answers about the big things as well. It was good to get a good night's sleep because the next day was Friday, deadline day.

Radio message from Dan Weaver, Branch Director:
March 4

Seymour and Jo Ann flew to Isabela this morning from Zamboanga City planning to go to Panigayan for some of Eunice's things. However, the trip to Panigayan was postponed by the return of a negotiating delegation. Seymour was given two letters from Eunice which he will deliver to authorities in Zamboanga. We have not been informed of the contents.

We have no further news. Negotiations continue.

Dr. Richard Pittman is arriving Friday from Indonesia. We will benefit from his wise counsel.

On a visit to Philippine Constabulary Headquarters yesterday I noticed a sign on the office wall, "Nothing is impossible". How much more true that is for us. I have been encouraged and strengthened by II Chronicles 20:15-30, particularly verses 17 and 22 (Living Bible).

Additional message:

Seymour has just given us some of the contents of the most recent notes from Eunice. Eunice did receive the medicines and Bible and other things sent earlier and greatly appreciated these. Eunice said medicines, which included Aralin, arrived just in time because the leader had come down with malaria. Eunice seems to have a good relationship with the people. Sulaiman was told he could go free but he chose to remain with Eunice. Eunice particularly appreciates Scriptures and mentioned they were a blessing.

Praise the Lord, she is well and in good spirits.

Friday, March 5

My captors had asked for the money to be brought by today, and I woke up feeling a bit apprehensive. I drew comfort once again from the Scriptures. It occurred to me that God is not in a hurry. I certainly was, I just wanted to get out of there! But I realised that perhaps God didn't want me out yet.

The Lord convicted me of anger. Reading Psalm 37:1-8 I realised that I was fretting because of the apparent control that my captors had over my situation, and I was angry at the things I had to put up with. I was tired of being stared at by groups of men, and even women, and not being able to get away from them. And I hated the daily ritual of having to ask permission to go to the toilet (actually, the bushes) and to have someone going with me. It was humiliating. But God showed me that anger was not the right reaction to all this, and I must stop it.

I spent some time thinking and wondering about the ransom. I reached Psalm 50 and in verses 9 and 10 God said, "I will take no bullock out of thy house, nor he-goats out of thy folds. For every beast of the forest is mine, and the cattle upon a thousand hills." And I believed that the Lord said to me through that, that He wouldn't take anything of mine. I knew it was impossible anyway, because I didn't have that much money. But if it had to be I could contribute something. Now the Lord definitely said He wasn't going to take anything from me. That was good.

For the first time since my capture, I was allowed to go to the stream to take a bath. Previously water had been brought to the house, but now they told me they were tired of carrying it. I was very glad. I was tired of staying in the house all the time! I was afraid I would never be able to walk again unless I got some exercise. Now I went with the girls to the stream to bathe and do some laundry. My bodyguard came along with me and amused himself by shooting at birds and just generally hanging around to make sure that I didn't run off anywhere. There was always someone responsible for keeping an eye on me in the house, and I was never allowed to leave the house without a companion. But this was the first time I was particularly conscious of my "bodyguard".

In the late afternoon, the female negotiator arrived for the second time, and I thought she looked worried. She brought a letter from Seymour and the things I had specifically asked for in my letter to Jo Ann. I was very pleased to have them. Now I would be able to keep a more detailed diary of events, and also write notes as I read the Scriptures. I smiled, too, as I discovered some verses of Scripture scribbled on the newspaper which wrapped up the notebook.

She had also brought two recent newspapers with her, and this, I was afraid, might be our undoing because they carried reports about the kidnapping. My captors read them, of course, and they were very angry. The newspaper articles quoted both Seymour and the British

Embassy as saying that they were very happy to leave everything in the hands of the military authorities. One of the first conditions that my captors had laid down was that the military should not be involved in any way. I felt a bit afraid and wondered what was going to happen because it was also deadline day and no ransom had been paid. Seymour's letter assured me that the military authorities were aware of the danger to me and would stay away. And he encouraged me: "Keep trusting God. He'll work it out well."

I prayed to the Lord again for a good night's sleep, and that night it seemed as if I was sleeping in a nice comfortable bed. It was fantastic! How good the Lord was in answering another little prayer.

Radio message from Dan Weaver, Branch Director: *March 5*

Very little new information to report. Seymour and Jo Ann are in Isabela. They went to Panigayan today to get Eunice's things. This was particularly hard both on Jo Ann and their family and friends on Panigayan. The people were saddened thinking perhaps the girls would not be coming back.

The government peace talks will be held on Basilan tomorrow and Sunday. This may have some significance in the negotiations. Please pray for this. I do not consider it wise for Seymour to attend or participate in this conference although he was invited to attend.

Large groups of people meeting in Horsleys Green, Great Britain, to remember Eunice. Huntington Beach (international headquarters in California) *has sent word to all branches so there are many intercessors. An interesting footnote is that Sulaiman helped Eunice translate the story of Joseph. They are now living through a similar experience. "God's faithfulness is unchanging and his good purposes will be fulfilled" Lamentations 3:21-26 (Living Bible). Hope and wait quietly with confidence.*

Saturday, March 6

Commander J– returned, so I had cause to feel a little apprehensive. But he was very friendly and asked me if I had read the newspaper articles and what I thought of them. "I don't know," was all I could reply. Then he said, "Let's play Scrabble". A few days before someone had produced a chess set and Scrabble so that I would have something to do. We started the game of Scrabble – just the two of us. He was a good player, but I had to smile to myself when he made words like "rebel" and "bad". I wondered how long this friendly approach would last. And should I play to win – I was in the lead – or let him win? Supper-time came and solved that problem – the game was abandoned.

The crunch came after supper, when he said, "Now you'll write a letter." His mood had changed and I could tell that he was angry. I was a bit upset as I wrote the letter:

Dear Seymour,

Thanks for your note. I'm encouraged by it but also discouraged. I've been told to write to you as follows:

Saturday, March 6

The MNLF is extremely angry that the military and government is involved and they refuse to negotiate with them. I am to tell you not to rely on them if you are concerned for my safe release. In fact they say that if the military/government negotiates they will *never* release me, but I'll be taken off to the interior of Zamboanga del Sur. They say this is *not* a bluff. They need the money and insist that it be paid by SIL and/or the British Embassy.

Seymour, they're not bluffing, I'm sure. They will only allow until *Monday, 8th March* now, and they want you to come here to Lamitan II with two companions as previously stated. They also say that no-one must be told that the money has been paid.

I don't know what you will do . . . may God give you His wisdom. "Power belongeth unto God." Psa. 62:11 – this is a comfort to me.

They think the government thinks they can be easily persuaded, and they intend to show that they can't be. That's all they have said, so I'll close, and trust this will reach you tomorrow as scheduled.

Love to Jo Ann, you and everyone,

EUNICE

I felt that they meant what they said. I really couldn't tell, of course, but it was frightening enough to believe, and I scribbled in my diary, "God help me, they mean it." This was the beginning of the hardest period of my time in captivity. I didn't sleep much that night.

Radio message from Dan Weaver, Branch Director:
March 6

> *No news to report today. Let us not grow weary in well-doing, nor weaken in our confidence and hope. I am glad to share Psalm 111 with you accompanied with 2 Chronicles 20:22 (Living Bible).*

Sunday, March 7

I woke up feeling sick at heart and apprehensive. In the morning I had to add a postcript to the letter. This time I was told the English words to write. Usually everything was said in Bangingi and I had to make my own version in English. They knew English very well, but I imagine they preferred to talk to me in Bangingi. I wrote:

> Seymour, they have just told me to tell you not to show this letter to the military/government. They say I will be harmed if the money isn't produced, and ask me to tell you to bring it as soon as possible, if you pity me. I repeat, if you really pity me, please bring the money, P200,000, yourself with the companions mentioned.

I hated writing this and imagined how Seymour would feel when he read it. After writing it I asked if I could go with the girls to the stream as usual, to bathe, and was told, "Yes, but after today you won't go out walking any more." My heart sank even lower.

It was a bad morning altogether. Everything seemed to be repulsive to me: the smell of the petrol as they cleaned their guns, the clicking noise as they loaded their guns;

everything and everybody. I really had to cry to the Lord about it. I was getting a bad attitude and it was going to be hard to carry on.

This was Sunday of course, so I wanted to spend extra time reading the Scriptures and praying. God reminded me that I was *not* alone in my predicament – other people were praying for me. I read in Psalm 54:4, "Behold, God is mine helper; the Lord is with them that uphold my soul." Of course! It's 8.50 a.m., everyone at Nasuli is meeting right now, and they're probably praying for me! As if to emphasize this point, Psalm 55:18 stood out to me, "He hath delivered my soul in peace from the battle that was against me: for there were many with me." Yes, people at home would be praying too, especially at Preston Chapel. I reached Psalm 56:3,4, "What time I am afraid I will trust in thee. In God I will praise his word, in God I have put my trust; I will not fear what flesh can do unto me." I memorised those verses and was helped and strengthened then and on many occasions in the days to come. "Trust God: don't be afraid of what mere human beings can do to you." Then I came to verse 9, "When I cry unto thee, then shall mine enemies turn back: this I know; for God is for me." I hardly dared believe that I could claim that promise. It was hard, because I had been crying to the Lord and I couldn't see any sign of my captors preparing to let me go. But I continued crying to the Lord on the basis of this word of His.

As I considered all this the thought came to me, "Do I insist on being released or am I willing, if it is God's will, that it be otherwise?" I wasn't willing. I remembered how my SIL colleague, Betty Hooker, had testified a year earlier about her experiences in the town of Lamitan, not so far from where I was now. On her own in the house, with gunfire outside, she had to ask herself if she could trust the Lord not only with her life, but also with her death. Now her experience helped me as I had to ask the same question. It was quite a struggle. I tried to sort out whether I was really willing not to be released, if that was what God wanted for me. Then I read the next Psalm, which was number 57, and was struck by verses 7–9: "My heart is fixed, O God, my heart is fixed. I will sing and give praise. Awake up, my glory; awake, psaltery and harp: I myself will awake early. I will praise thee, O Lord, among the people: I will sing unto thee among the nations." Here was the answer. "If I will praise the Lord like that, it will really delight His heart." So I did. The Lord enabled me to sing and to praise Him and I knew victory. The struggle was over. It would be all right with me whether God wanted to release me or not. I felt at peace the rest of that day. I spent my time inside the room, thinking about the Lord. He reminded me of the song in Isaiah 55:12: "For ye shall go out with joy, and be led forth with peace: the mountains and the hills shall break forth before you into singing, and all the trees of the field shall clap their hands." That song already had a deep meaning for me, and all of a sudden it came to mind again and took on a different significance. "Go out . . . to what? Be led forth . . . to what?" No matter what, it would be with inner joy and peace of mind and heart. And God's creation would rejoice with me too. What a prospect!

In the afternoon, it suddenly seemed that this joyful prospect might become an immediate reality. A different negotiator arrived. I could hear someone talking with the men out on the verandah and could understand what they were saying. After a while I was told I should go out on the verandah. I went out, and saw that the negotiator was wearing a turban, so he was obviously a *hadji,* one who has made the pilgrimage to Mecca. I didn't know him and he didn't know me, so he proceeded to ask me some questions. He asked me to explain about our work. He asked if I had been molested by my captors, and I told him I hadn't. And then he appealed to the two commanders to let him take me back to Zamboanga City. The purpose of his visit was to try and effect an exchange between me and a relative of his, who was also a relative of Commander J–. This man, H–, had been held in jail ever since the kidnapping of a Japanese woman the previous August. He had now been let out of jail into the *hadji's* custody, in order for this exchange to be made. H–'s mother and a brother had come along too. The *hadji* made a very impassioned plea to the two commanders. I could understand almost everything he said. He even wept as he begged to be able to take me back. But they weren't willing. They tried to stall, saying, "We want to have some papers. It couldn't possibly be settled today. We'd have to go and do this or that." The *hadji* said, "Even if it's tomorrow or the day after, I'll wait." They said, "All right." So the visitors prepared to stay the night.

My captors went straight off to have a conference somewhere, leaving one man behind to guard me.

While they were away, two letters arrived for me. One was a short note from Jo Ann assuring me of everyone's prayers, and listing some Scripture passages to read. The other was from Betty Hooker's co-worker, Dietlinde Behrens, and it was torn into six pieces and very crumpled. After piecing it together I could read it fairly easily, and was encouraged by the Scripture verses she quoted. I found out later that Dietlinde had sent some glucose tablets with her letter, but these never reached me. However, I looked forward to letters more than anything else.

The family had a good time that evening. It was moonlight and the young people went down outside the house to do Muslim dancing and to play the *kulingtangan*, a musical instrument consisting of five round brass pieces and played with hammers like a xylophone. Everyone seemed to be very happy. I felt happy too! It was nice that somebody had come . . . somebody who was going to stay.

Radio Message from Dan Weaver, Branch Director:
March 7

Government peace-talks are being held on Basilan today. They may be very crucial in negotiations for Eunice's release. Pray for the authorities. Pray for continued strength and good health for Seymour and the girls. For your strength and encouragement, Psalm 91.

Monday, March 8

Very early in the morning most of the men went off to discuss what was going to happen. The radio had been on all day continuously since the previous Wednesday, but today it was silent so the atmosphere was much better for reading and praying.

Our SIL Director in Manila, Dan Weaver, had recommended via Seymour's second letter that I read Psalm 116. I had read it before, and had wondered about verse 15, "Precious in the sight of the Lord is the death of his saints." Did it mean that I was going to die? But today as I read it I also had the Living Bible version in mind, which Seymour quoted in his letter. "His loved ones are very precious to Him and He does not lightly let them die." That was an encouragement to me and I knew God had allowed this to happen for a purpose. I realised it was a privilege to be entrusted with a small measure of suffering for the Lord's sake, but I felt that deliverance was near and that I would live.

During the day I overheard a conversation mentioning a ransom sum of 80,000 pesos (about £6,000). Nothing was said to me directly about it, of course, but I was put under some pressure by H–'s mother as to why SIL had not produced the P200,000 as demanded. She assured me that they were helping me and that they were there to try and get me released. But we would have to come up with the money and why didn't we? Many times she spoke to me like this. I had to tell her that I too didn't know why nothing was happening. I had written the letters and I couldn't really do anything else from my end.

Overhearing the talk about the ransom-money reminded me again of the Lord's promise that He wouldn't take anything from me. I had another reminder too – not to put my trust in men. It was nice when the *hadji* was there. It gave me a feeling of security, and that perhaps I would be released fairly soon. I read in Psalm 60:11, "Give us help from trouble: for vain is the help of man." It was a reminder not to put my trust in the *hadji*, but only in God. That prepared me for what was coming, because later on in the day, they all went home and I was left behind, not really surprised, but a little disappointed.

Before they left, I was asked to write a note to the Colonel requesting him please to meet the demands of the MNLF, so that I could be released before too long. I wrote the note and the *hadji* took it back. My captors told me later in the evening that I would go home the next day, when the *hadji* came back with the money. But I had no assurance that it was going to be so.

My stomach had been feeling a bit upset all day and I hoped it didn't mean that my old problem of amoeba was flaring up again. I took some of the medicine Seymour had sent and it seemed to help. "Thank you, Lord, for this medicine." I also thanked the Lord for the house I was living in, since the weather became wet and colder. And I asked Him to keep me warm. It was often a little chilly at night anyway, but tonight would be worse. There was nothing else I could put on since I always wore most of my clothes at night. God cares about little things – He answered my prayer and kept me warm.

Tuesday, March 9

I wondered what today would hold. As I continued reading the Psalms, God assured me that He had already provided me with sufficient strength for this day, whatever happened – Psalm 68: 28: "Thy God hath commanded thy strength . . ." I was convinced, too, that God would bring me out, and that there would be an end of the embarrassment and humiliation I often felt. I would certainly have much to praise Him for when the day came – somehow I didn't think it would be today.

Nearly everybody had gone to the beach very early in the morning to wait for the arrival of the *hadji*. A little after midday, H–'s mother and brother arrived in a hurry, running up to the house and saying, "Ed is being attacked. He's down there at the mosque. You'd better go!" (I don't know who "Ed" was – whether it was the name of one of my captors, or someone else.) We had heard shooting some minutes earlier but we often did, so we hadn't thought anything of it until now. Commander J– rushed out of the house saying, "If somebody has come to attack us, we will slash the 'Americano' with our bolos."

"Oh God, no, not the bolo! I'd rather be shot if I have to die! But I don't want to die . . . Help, Lord!" Some time ago they had showed me an extra long and sharp bolo which could be used for killing people. (Smaller varieties of the knife were usually worn at the side and used for jobs in the house and fields.) The other women in the house were alarmed, too, and we all waited nervously for the men to return. Then we discovered that it had only been somebody shooting down young coconuts from a tree. A false alarm!

H–'s mother brought me a few more items sent by Seymour, including a bottle of aspirins, and another bottle of rubbing alcohol, for both of which there was a great demand. The *hadji* didn't come back. At least he didn't come to the house. He may have come as far as the shore, talked to my captors and returned to Zamboanga. When I enquired they told me he was afraid to come again. Later on I heard that he had actually made five trips, but I saw him only twice, including the day I was released.

In the mid-afternoon my captors told me they were sending Sulaiman home that day and I was to write a letter for him to take. This time they brought a box for me to use as a table, and both my captors and the family sat around as I was told the contents of the letter:

DEAR SEYMOUR,

I am sending Sulaiman to you with this message.

> Please send P150,000 [1] here with Sulaiman tomorrow, 10th March. This will be the last letter I will write, because if the money doesn't arrive tomorrow I will be killed. I believe this to be true. Sulaiman has been released so that he can take this message to you and bring the money back. Please try to help me. It *must* be tomorrow.
>
> With my love to you all,
> EUNICE

God did a lovely thing for me as I wrote that letter. As I listened to my captors telling me to write, "I will be killed", the words flashed into my mind, "I shall not die but live."[2] I wasn't even sure that those words were in the Scriptures, but I supposed they must be since the Lord had brought them into my mind. So that as I wrote the words, "I will be killed", I felt perfectly calm – just as if I was actually writing, "I shall not die but live."

I was also told to write on the back of the letter in the Bangingi language; here is an approximate translation:

> I will be killed if the money does not arrive tomorrow. Help me, look for money with which to pay the ransom, you too, dear older sister. The Colonel is not helping me. Thank you, my brothers and sisters. Hurry and send the money here with Sulaiman tomorrow, P150,000.
>
> EUNICE

After I'd written the letter, everybody gathered sympathetically around. Then I didn't feel quite so good, and wept a bit. My diary recorded: "Do they really mean to

[1] about £11,500

[2] Psalm 118:17

kill me?" I couldn't tell. I felt a bit downcast, even though the Lord had given me a promise that I would live. Reading on in the Psalms I found myself asking again with the psalmist, "How long?" This was the third disappointment ... yet when I read Psalm 77:7-9 I wrote, "Has God forgotten or forsaken me? No!" I read on ... "Thou art the God that doest wonders ..." [1] Yes, not only for the people of Israel hundreds of years ago, but *for me now*! I had experienced much of the grace and power of God in my life during the thirteen years since my conversion in 1963. He had challenged me with the need for Bible translation work and led me to give up my job in order to train to be a Bible translator. He had enabled me to complete two years at Redcliffe Missionary Training College, two summers at the SIL School in England and five months of jungle training camp in Mexico. When I asked Him which country to go to He had clearly led me to the Philippines. He had asked me to trust only Himself for the supply of my financial needs and He had given me more than I had believed possible. Thinking back over these things encouraged me to trust Him now in this trying situation.

The events of the day weren't yet over. I had been enjoying wearing Commander S–'s big watch, and was planning to give it to Sulaiman as a thank-you present when I was released. But now two men came to "borrow" it. In spite of what they said I felt sure that I would never see it again – and I never have.

H–'s mother and brother were staying in the house with us again. At first I had liked having them around but now I found the pressure almost too much to bear. Always the same old question, "Why doesn't Seymour Ashley bring the money?" Why not indeed?

[1] Ps 77:14

During the evening I was told to go out on to the verandah. Commanders J– and H– were there and they started to tell me, "When you go home to Zamboanga, this is what you should tell the Colonel." I thought, "It doesn't sound as if they are going to kill me, not quite yet, anyway." I slept well that night.

Radio message from Dan Weaver, Branch Director:
March 9

I leave in a few minutes for Manila after spending Monday and Tuesday in Zamboanga City. I am confident that everything possible is being done to obtain the release of Eunice.

Seymour is doing an absolutely heroic job in maintaining contacts and relationships with the authorities.

Jo Ann returned to Nasuli this morning. There was no emergency, we simply felt it was best for her to await Eunice's release at Nasuli.

Don't give up in your prayer efforts for Eunice and everyone associated. Continue to take courage in the fact that God is in control. Read Isaiah 45: 5-13 (Living Bible).

Wednesday, March 10

I had a very heavy heart. I tried to read the Scriptures as usual but they seemed to be closed – it was as if I couldn't make contact with God. I considered: "Suppose this is my last day on this earth . . . how do I want to spend it? Not in feeling sorry for myself! I should pray and read the Scriptures, even if they do seem to be closed." So I persevered in reading. Then this verse seemed to be for me: "Let the sighing of the prisoner come before thee; according to the greatness of thy power preserve thou those that are appointed to die" (Psalm 79:11). This was my prayer too. God also spoke to me through Psalm 81. The first few verses reminded me that God expected me to praise Him, even if I didn't feel like it. So I sang hymns and psalms of praise to myself. Reading on, I came to those verses where God says His people wouldn't listen to Him so He let them have their own way, but His way would have been much better. Once again I told the Lord that I did want His way because it would be better, whichever way it went. It occurred to me, "All these psalms of deliverance are such a comfort and help but I'm not completely convinced they are for me. Perhaps I should read in some other part of the Scriptures." I had been thinking how lovely it would be to come home to all my friends and colleagues, to have a human welcome as it were. But, "How about if it's a *divine* welcome that I get when I go home? That should be even better. Am I prepared for it?" So I started reading in the Book of Revelation, and was comforted to realize what it would be like to be welcomed by the Lord.

The time seemed to drag even more now that I had no watch. The family noticed that my watch had gone, and as soon as the last of my captors went off to the shore they all gathered round to ask about it. We relaxed a bit, talked and ate bananas while they were gone.

The day wore on and nobody came. Sulaiman obviously hadn't come back as instructed. I wondered if he was having trouble finding Seymour and Jo Ann. What if they had left Isabela and were waiting for me in Zamboanga City? How would Sulaiman find them? What about the ransom? Part of me wished that somebody would pay it so that I could get out of there. I thought about my family – perhaps they would prefer that it be paid somehow, so that they could have me back with them alive and well. Then the Lord led me to ask myself, "Would it really be right to use the Lord's money to save one of His children from an early meeting with Him?" When I looked at it like that, it clearly wasn't right.

It was late when my captors finally returned from the shore. They sat on the verandah for a long time, talking in low tones. Nothing was said to me, so I didn't have anything particular to worry about that night, and I slept well.

Thursday, March 11

I reminded myself again to seek and accept God's way because it was going to be the best and it would be the only way of blessing. Before I had a chance to go for my daily bath, Commander J– said, "Let's play Scrabble." There were four of us playing this time. Commander J– said, "If you win, you can go home, even if they don't send any money." I thought, "He's joking of course. But it's too good an offer to miss. I'd really better try and win, just in case he means it."

We played and I was doing quite well for a while. Then somebody got a good score and raced ahead and I was lagging behind. I tried to improve my score but it was getting near the end of the game and there weren't many letters left. "I'll never win now" . . . but I did! I put all my letters out first and they had to deduct their left-overs which were then added to my score. So I won after all, but as usual, after a time of being particularly friendly, there was a crunch coming soon afterwards.

I went down to bathe with the girls and we were just getting ready to go back to the house, when the men came down to the stream. Commander J– shot off his gun in our vicinity, scattering the leaves near us. It frightened all of us. He said, "If Sulaiman doesn't come today, you'll be killed." I returned to the house and read some more and drew more comfort from the Psalms. There were the lovely verses 14 and 15 of Psalm 91: "Because he hath set his love upon me, therefore will I deliver him . . . he shall call upon me, and I will answer him: I will be with him in trouble; I will deliver him, and honour him." I wanted to be able to claim all those promises; I knew what the Lord had already said to me, but it was awfully hard to be very confident. I was in dire straits. This was a matter of life or death. To trust completely in God now demanded an exercise of faith greater than I had known so far in my Christian life. I felt like the man who cried to Jesus, "Lord, I believe; help thou mine unbelief" (Mark 9:24). I realised I couldn't make Sulaiman come with the money, but I really thought he would come. I didn't know how much of what my captors said I should believe, but thought, "If Sulaiman realises the contents of that letter and thinks they mean it, he'll be back here, even if he doesn't bring any money." But I knew I couldn't do anything about it; whether he would come or not, I had to leave it to the Lord.

If he didn't come, it seemed that there were probably two alternatives: I might be killed, or I might be taken off to the "jungle" of Zamboanga del Sur which my captors had mentioned several times.

I had another struggle, and thought especially of my family – my mother and father, my dear sister, Phyllis, my brother, Vincent, and his two children, Sarah and Nicholas. How I longed to see them all again! Then I realised that even if my captors killed me, perhaps the Lord would use that to bring my family to really know Him. Then we would all meet each other in heaven, and that would be better than meeting down here.

Later in the afternoon, Commander J– poked his head in the door and said, "Pack your things." Pack . . . for what? To die? To move? To go home? My heart was in turmoil for a while. Then I packed my box. I packed everything. I had already planned that if I was going home I would leave behind certain things and give them to the family – clothes, medicines, mosquito-net. But I was sure I wasn't going home today. And in spite of what my captors had said, I didn't feel that I was going to be killed either. I thought I would probably be taken to Zamboanga del Sur, and I would need all my things there. I wrapped them in a large plastic bag that I had, so that they wouldn't get wet on the boat ride, and tied them up in my box. God gave me peace.

Then I sat on the porch talking to H–'s brother and mother who were still there. "Where am I going?" I asked. They replied, "You're going to the house of another commander. Everyone is going off to another island for the Maulud celebration." Maulud was a Muslim festival which was being held that night. So I asked, "When am I going?" "Tomorrow," the mother answered but the son immediately said, "No, to-night." I thought it would probably be that night since they usually liked to move people around under cover of darkness. So there was probably going to be another walk ahead . . . I hadn't walked very far recently. My daily trip to the stream and back took only about four minutes each way. I needed to claim the Lord's strength for the journey.

After supper I was told to rest for a while. Then at about eight o'clock we set off. I claimed God's promise in Philippians 4:13, "I can do all things through Christ which strengtheneth me." Yes, God would surely give me the strength for this walk, however far it would be. I repeated this verse often and also sang it to myself as we went along.

First we went down to the coast, a walk of perhaps three-quarters of an hour. We waited for a while beside a little group of houses, then I was handed over to my new custodians, and we walked inland for about another three-quarters of an hour.

These people were Yakans, members of a Muslim group whose language is closely related to Bangingi. There were three of them, one commander and his two companions. As we walked along one of these two asked in Bangingi, "What's your name?" "My name is Eunice." They said, "Oh, you're Eunice. What's the other girl's name?" "Jo Ann." "Oh yes," then the man started singing a little song about Jo Ann and me which our friends sing in Panigayan. "That's strange, how does he know that song?" I wondered, and commented, "Oh, you know that song." He said, "Yes, I'm often in Panigayan." It turned out that he sometimes stayed in one of the Bangingi homes there and that's where he had heard about us and learned the song.

It must have been about 10 o'clock when we finally got to my new home – a big wooden house on stilts, with a metal roof. We went in and the two young women and one fellow left in the house woke up and came to greet us. The women prepared to cook the fish my companions had brought with them, but I didn't want to eat anything. They showed me where I was going to sleep which was inside a smallish room on my own. There were a mat and a pillow on the floor, and I had brought the blanket with me from the other house.

The whole night long there was gunfire going on all around and I couldn't sleep. "Where have they brought me?" I wondered. "I didn't know there was any battle going on. Have they brought me into a fighting zone?"

Radio message from Dan Weaver, Branch Director:
March 11

We have just received word from Seymour that Sulaiman has been released and is in Zamboanga City. He is well. Sulaiman brought a letter from Eunice dated, Tuesday, March 9. We do not know the contents but the general tone of the letter seems good. Seymour says that most certainly the emotional strain of this long time will be severe and we must continue to uphold her.

Looking only at circumstances our hope can go up and down like a yo-yo. Remember, our trust is in God.

Friday, March 12

When I asked about the gunfire, one of them said, "That was just the Maulud celebration. There isn't any battle going on around here. You're safer here than you were in the other place." My feelings were, "I might be safer, but I don't think I'm going to like it here." Living arrangements at the other house hadn't been too bad, and I had enjoyed being with the girls of the family. And the house had been clean. This house was dirty, and the two young women seemed immature and irresponsible. How would I get on with them?

The room I had slept in had a doorway but no door. Before long,the Commander appeared with a door, hinges and nails, and within minutes had hammered the door into place. "We don't want anyone to see you," he explained. So I was to be shut up in this room . . . Well, it was perhaps a little bigger than the one at the other house; it had a window with wooden louvres so wasn't too dark. I would be able to read and pray. And it certainly would be nice not to be seen – I was tired of being looked at all the time. I thought again of other people like the Millers, who had to spend their time in the open, and I counted my blessings.

There were more questions from the Commander, who seemed to be a mild sort of fellow, very reasonable, and not at all in agreement with the kidnapping. He said the people who kidnapped me were different and the MNLF didn't agree with it. He felt sure I would be going home soon.

People were coming and going all the morning, so I stayed hidden in my room, and ate my meals there. As I continued reading in the Psalms I reached Psalm 93:4, and I felt sure that God would prove His mighty power to me. Then I read Psalm 94 and verse 14 stood out: "For the Lord will not cast off His people, neither will He forsake His inheritance." I wrote in my notebook "This is a promise – I *know* God has not forsaken me."

In the afternoon I was allowed to leave my room and go with the girls to the stream to take a bath. They had some shampoo and I revelled in the luxury of washing my hair with shampoo for the first time in two weeks. Previously I had just poured water over it every day. They had plenty of laundry soap, and we used this for bathing, too. They said it stopped them getting itchy skin but I found that constant use turned my arms a strange colour – almost as if my skin had been bleached. Because I wasn't to be seen, we had to play a few games of hide-and-seek, on the way to and from the stream. If anybody was in sight I had to hide behind a tree or at least make myself look more the height of a Filipino and not an "Americano". When we got back to the house they told me I was free to sit in the kitchen or on the verandah as long as no-one else was around. But as soon as anyone approached the house I was to run inside my room and fasten the door. So I wasn't going to be a prisoner in my little room after all!

The house had belonged to a *hadji* who had fled because of fighting in the area, and some of his furniture had been left behind. There were chairs! Oh the joy of sitting on a chair again – I really was tired of sitting on the floor. There were two upright chairs and a wooden settee and armchairs, and I sat in them at every possible opportunity. There was no table, but they had placed two large wooden boxes together and sat around them to eat.

From that evening onwards I ate with everyone else, as long as no visitors were around. The household consisted of the Commander, with long curly hair, past shoulder-length; his wife, with short straight hair, only 21 years old, and her 16-year-old sister, who had been brought from the town of Lamitan to be my companion. Then there were usually two or three other MNLF soldiers in the house. They were all very friendly, and I began to feel much more relaxed and "at home" here, despite my first impressions of the place. I really enjoyed my food, and this delighted them. They were very concerned that I should eat well so that I wouldn't get sick. They wouldn't be able to get any medicine and they didn't want me to die on them. And the food was good. Since there were fewer people to feed we usually had a lot more fish or vegetables each than at the other house.

I felt encouraged by their attitude. They really seemed anxious that I should go home. And they said that if any money was to be paid, it should be paid by the government, not by SIL or me. The Commander felt that asking for money from SIL, as an organisation, was hitting at someone they didn't want to hit at. They should be demanding it from the government.

Saturday, March 13

The younger sister of the Commander's wife slept in the room with me last night. The two of us fitted nicely on the mat and under the mosquito net. She was a very sweet Yakan girl, and I came to love her and her sister. They were great fun to be with, making the atmosphere in the house very relaxed. It was so different here. In the other house I never felt very free to talk to the women because I had discovered that everything I said was reported to the fellows afterwards. That had been embarrassing on occasions. But here, there was no one to report to – such a relief. I could recover a bit from the strain of the past two weeks.

Since I was hidden inside my room for much of the time, there was more opportunity to read and pray. As I read today I thought the Lord gave me a verse for all of our SIL workers in the Philippines. Psalm 97:1: "The Lord reigneth; let the earth rejoice; let the multitude of isles be glad thereof." There's a multitude of islands in the Philippines and I felt God was promising that all our workers in those islands would soon be rejoicing as they saw God's power evidenced in my release.

I was very glad of the privacy of the closed door, but there were disadvantages. Sometimes I had to wait for hours before being allowed out to go to the toilet and there were days when I couldn't go out for my daily bath. The girls would usually manage to slip a cup of tea or a meal in to me, though.

There had been a school in the area, which was now abandoned, and a box of books from the school lay underneath the house. The Commander's wife, her sister and some of the fellows enjoyed reading them. They would sit around in their spare time reading out loud. I liked listening to them. Some of the books were in Tagalog, the national language of the Philippines, and some were in English. I was glad of something else to read, too, and spent time poring over the Tagalog books, trying to brush up my knowledge of that language.

My small copy of the New Testament and Psalms interested one of the young fellows. He asked to borrow it for a while, and took it away to read, but found the English too hard to understand. When he returned he asked me to explain a couple of verses. I was delighted to try to do so. I remembered one of my captors at the first house who had also borrowed the book and who had asked if he could have it when I went home. Why did he want it? Just to have something to read? To improve his English? Or to find out what God had to say to him?

The days were passing and there was no sign that anything was happening. The Commander went to the shore every day to wait for news, and every evening he came home and reported that nobody had arrived. It was also a week now since I had received any letters . . .

Sunday, March 14

My third Sunday in captivity. I enjoyed a time of singing. It was possible to sing out loud here, as long as I did it softly. "Praise the Saviour, ye who know Him" was a hymn that always lifted my heart to the Lord in praise and worship, and I sang it often. As for the fears that would come from time to time, they were dispelled by calling to mind His promises in the words of another hymn:

> Fear not, I am with thee, O be not dismayed;
> For I am thy God, and will still give thee aid:
> I'll strengthen thee, help thee, and cause thee to stand
> Upheld by My righteous, omnipotent hand.

As I read this morning I found myself asking with the psalmist: "O when wilt thou come unto me?" (Psalm 101:2). It seemed that God's answer came in Psalm 102:13: "Thou shalt arise, and have mercy upon Zion: for the time to favour her, yea, the set time, is come." "So there's a set time for my deliverance . . . has it come?"

One of the fellows in the house had poor eyesight, and had it in mind to borrow my glasses. I was by now used to people wanting to try them on, and knew that he would soon hand them back as the others had. For the first time in my life I was glad that I needed such strong lenses! No-one wanted to keep them! I thanked the Lord for this – and found out later that a friend at Nasuli had been specifically praying that my glasses wouldn't be taken away. The Lord answered both our prayers.

The mosquitoes were particularly bad at this house in the late afternoon and early evening, so I started to retreat under my mosquito-net during those hours. Yesterday I had been bitten all over my arms. It was hot under the net – I wished that Seymour and Jo Ann had thought to send some insect repellent. Later on I found out that they had in fact sent some along with other things in a box which didn't reach me.

When the Commander came home from the shore he brought us Coca-Cola drinks and biscuits, and a new tube of toothpaste for me. Little things, but what an encouragement!

Monday, March 15

The house was very active, with people coming and going, and I was in my room for much of the day.

The Lord spoke to me through Psalm 105:43, "And he brought forth his people with joy, and his chosen with gladness". My heart leaped as I realised the Lord was going to bring me forth. I found myself singing once more the words of Isaiah 55:12, "For ye shall go out with joy, and be led forth with peace: the mountains and the hills shall break forth before you into singing, and all the trees of the field shall clap their hands." But the Lord pulled me up short as I read on . . . Psalm 106: 13-15: ". . . they waited not for his counsel . . . and he gave them their request; but sent leanness into their soul." My diary recorded: "I don't want this (leanness of soul) so let me not be in a hurry to get out of here if God has more to do in me yet."

I resumed memorising Scripture. I had been reading a lot and memorising odd verses, but the passage I had been memorising before I'd been kidnapped, Romans chapter 6, hadn't seemed applicable to my present situation, so I hadn't continued with it. But today I decided to continue and go on into chapters 7 and 8.

A group of seven men arrived that afternoon, and once it became clear that they were going to stay the night I was allowed out of the room. I could not be hidden for that length of time. As always I was struck by their appearance, especially the long hair which seemed to mark allegiance to the MNLF. Many of them could easily be mistaken for girls.

After the relative protection of my closed door it was somewhat of a shock to be exposed to the remarks of a group of men again, and I found myself near to tears as they commented to each other. Their language was similar enough to Bangingi for me to understand much of what was said. The girls were sympathetic, however, and the next time such conversation seemed to be starting they said "Don't! She'll cry!" It worked – there was no more such talk, and I was thankful.

Radio Message from Dan Weaver, Branch Director: *March 15*

We have just received word from Seymour that he has

talked with relatives of those holding Eunice who have informed Seymour that Eunice is O.K. Praise the Lord for this encouraging word.
Negotiations are continuing and going well so please do not lose heart. Ephesians 3: 13-21 (Living Bible).

Tuesday, March 16

This was the first day I was really hungry. After a boiled banana for breakfast, we ate rice and a little fish at 9.30 a.m. Then all the men left. We girls spent two hours at the stream, bathing and doing our laundry – there was no question of having a bodyguard here! It was going to be 7.30 p.m. before we had another meal, when the Commander came home with the fish. That's when I discovered why I hadn't eaten at noon – there was no fish and they never thought of offering me just rice.

The Lord gave me a beautiful meditation on the fruit of the Spirit and how all the different fruit could be manifested in my life in my present situation. I wrote it down:

love	–	to be shown to my captors and those around me
joy	–	inner joy in spite of my circumstances
peace	–	of mind and heart, not worried
longsuffering	–	when their conversation offends me, when they stare at me
gentleness	–	in my attitude and speech to them

goodness	–	towards God and them – no evil thoughts
faith	–	that God will deliver me in His time
meekness	–	submissive attitude towards them, respect their temporary authority over me
temperance/ self-control	–	in eating, resting etc., but especially control of my emotions so that I won't weep

In the evening the Commander told me that Commander J– and all his men had left the other house and he didn't know where they were. I was disturbed to hear that. I didn't know whether it was good news or bad news. Had they all gone off and abandoned me?

That night there were only four of us in the house. The group of seven had left and the other fellows had gone to harvest coconuts, leaving only the Commander with the three of us girls. For the first time I didn't feel very safe. The Commander's wife had told me earlier that her husband didn't know how to use firearms. If he had to fight, he just used a bolo. I knew there wasn't a torch in the house either. No, I didn't feel very safe after having the security of all those guns . . .

Wednesday, March 17

I felt discouraged today at the apparent lack of communication from Commander J–. Could it really be that nothing was happening? I realized that I needed to encourage myself in the Lord. "Psalm 93:4 *is true,* no matter what the circumstances look like," I wrote. God's Word to me as I read the Scriptures was "Wait!" I had turned back to Psalm 25 which Jo Ann had mentioned in one of her letters. In verse 5 I read, "Lead me in Thy truth, and teach me: for Thou art the God of my salvation; on Thee do I WAIT all the day". And as I thought about this the words of a song based on Psalm 37:4 and 7 came into my mind: "O rest in the Lord, WAIT patiently for Him, and he shall give thee thy heart's desire". The message was repeated in Psalm 27:13 and 14: "I had fainted, unless I had believed to see the goodness of the Lord in the land of the living. WAIT on the Lord: be of good courage, and he shall strengthen thine heart: WAIT, I say, on the Lord." The remedy for my fainting heart was to trust God and wait.

I seemed to be brought out on view more. People were obviously getting to know I was there and more groups of soldiers were coming through. I was apparently being hidden from the civilians in the neighbourhood but not from the soldiers.

Later in the day, the commander of the group that had stayed the night was brought back. He had encountered a Philippine Constabulary patrol and had been shot in the wrist, which was now very swollen. They had their own medical equipment, including tetanus shots. I was told to go out and have a look while he was being treated. It upset me a bit to see him. I was relieved that I wasn't expected to do anything for him. His companion obviously had medical training, and soon the wounded man was walking around as good as new.

I started feeling apprehensive again, and wondered why. In the late afternoon I found out. I was told: "Commander J– is coming". I hadn't seen him for a week.

"Will it be bad news? O Lord, please help me not to be afraid." He came in and was very pleasant. He said he was willing to exchange me for H–, but Commander S– insisted on the payment of a ransom, however small. "Will you write to Mr. Ashley and just request . . . what do you think? . . . say, 10,000 pesos (about £770)." "Yes, I'll write that." He pursued the matter, "What do you think, can it be paid?" "I don't know," I replied, "but I'll write." I pondered the matter. "P10,000 isn't so bad. I have some money of my own – not that much, but with a bit of help I could probably scrape it together!" So I wrote the letter to Seymour and added, "I'm willing to pay this out of my own resources." Later that evening I remembered that the Lord had told me He wouldn't take anything of mine. Now what had I done? I shouldn't have written that . . . But the Lord overruled, for the letter was never delivered!

Commander J– seemed anxious that I should have a good impression of him. He asked me if I held any grudge against him. I said "no" but added that I had sometimes been afraid of him. "Yes," he said, "that was Commander S–'s idea. He insisted that we frighten you." Then he told me that their Commander-in-Charge would be coming to see me later.

H– and the other fellows had come with Commander J–. H– said to me in English, "Everybody is suffering because of you!" He exerted pressure again for payment of ransom, however small. The other men told me that relatives of H–'s were being held by the Colonel, so that explained his outburst.

My captors had brought a letter from Jerry and Joanna Otis, who are in charge of the Christian and Missionary Alliance guest house in Zamboanga City. I had often stayed with them there. The gist of their letter was, "Soon you'll be released. It's going to be so nice to see you." I was encouraged and wrote in my diary: "Perhaps it won't be long now . . ."

Thursday, March 18

"Another day in which to praise Him", reads my notebook. Yes, and to trust Him, too. I felt that God was working everything out according to His plan, so much higher than mine. Leaving the Psalms for once I read through the book of Philippians, and was very impressed by Chapter 1, verse 29: "For unto you it is given in the behalf of Christ, not only to believe on Him, but also to suffer for His sake". I realised again that it was a privilege to suffer a little for Him. Why had I been given this privilege? God knew – perhaps I would also know in time.

The household had run out of tea again, so we drank hot water for breakfast. Both households had been very considerate towards me, in always serving me hot drinks or cold bottled drinks. I had explained to them that I couldn't drink unboiled spring water because of the risk of further amoeba infection. God had indeed protected me and granted me good health. I was very thankful.

I had to stay in my room most of the day because a fellow arrived who they said had been captured by Commander J. It didn't seem to me that he was being held captive, since he was free to wander around the house and was left alone in the house with the women, when all the men went out. But they suspected him of being an intelligence agent and so they didn't want him talking to me. When it was decided that he would stay overnight, I was allowed out. He saw me, but didn't speak. That night the men brought all their guns into our bedroom because it had a door; they were afraid this fellow might grab one of the guns during the night and shoot us all.

The Yakan commander whose responsibility I was had told me previously that he would really like to send me home, but if he did, and Commander J– came back and found me gone, they would all be killed. This evening he came in with his wife and said, "You're going to go home!" And his wife laughing, said, "Yes, you might go home tomorrow, or if not, the day after." They said, "The ransom will be paid at P20,000 (about £1,500)." I thought, "I just wrote a letter suggesting P10,000. What's going to happen now?" Still, I was excited . . . but not as excited as they were. After all, I had been disappointed before. I hoped it was true, but I'd better not bank on it.

Radio Message from Dan Weaver, Branch Director:
March 18

There have been some new developments in the negotiations for Eunice's release which will hopefully have some positive results. Seymour is coming to Manila tonight to discuss these developments with me and returning to Zamboanga tomorrow. Please pray diligently for Seymour and for all concerned. God is able.

Friday, March 19

It rained in the night. I heard it and my heart sank, but I reminded myself that God knows best. I had been instructed to get up early and go straight to the stream to bathe. As I returned to the house it began to rain heavily again. I pictured a small pumpboat coming from Zamboanga City – a two-hour journey – and decided that they probably would not come because of the rain. But I sorted out my belongings, made a pile of things to leave behind for the girls and packed the rest in my box. Then I sat down to wait.

I'd reached Psalm 116 now, so read it once more, and this time was sure that deliverance had come and that I would live. Then it was 1.30 p.m. and no-one had arrived. I felt a bit disappointed, but remembered that God had a set time for my deliverance and His timing was best. Now I was reading Psalm 118, and was thrilled to find the verse that the Lord had brought to my mind when I had been threatened with death – verse 17: "I shall not die, but live, and declare the works of the Lord." "Not only will I live – I'll also be able to tell others what He has done for me!" It didn't matter if I had to wait another day or two – "This is the day which the Lord hath made; we will rejoice and be glad in it (v.24)." Rejoice! Don't waste the day indulging in self-pity or disappointment.

There had been nothing to eat again at noon, and I was hungry. At about two o'clock the girls asked, "Would you like a cup of tea?" I asked if there was anything to eat. They were apologetic: "There isn't anything to go with the rice." "Never mind," I answered, "I'll just eat rice." It tasted very good, too.

Two special visitors came to see me. The first one explained to me at great length the beliefs of the Muslim religion, and expressed the hope that I would consider embracing them myself. I in turn was able to share some of my beliefs. The second visitor explained once more the reason for my kidnapping. I don't know if either of these men was the Commander-in-Charge referred to by Comander J– – no-one was ever introduced to me as such.

I felt very relaxed in the afternoon and evening, in spite of the fact that we were quite a houseful. Lots of people were staying overnight. As I unpacked my box the familiar phrase came to mind, "Prepare for one more night." Surely it would only be one more . . .

Saturday, March 20

I awoke to a bright, sunny morning and the prospects looked good. But would anyone come for me today? Rather than be disappointed again I decided not to pack my things.

The Lord gave me the verse, Psalm 119:126: "It is time for Thee, Lord, to work . . ." and I felt sure the time had come. Reading on I came to Psalm 126:1-3: "When the Lord turned again the captivity of Zion, we were like them that dream. Then was our mouth filled with laughter, and our tongue with singing; then said they among the heathen, the Lord hath done great things for them. The Lord hath done great things for us; whereof we are glad." I thought, "This is the day!"

And so it was. We got word about 11.15 a.m. that my transport had arrived: two speedboats. The girls whooped for joy and said, "You're going home!" I started to get my things together. But before I could pack, the Yakan Commander came back with another fellow, who said, "Let's go and talk." After chatting for a few minutes he suddenly seemed embarrassed. "I hardly know how to say this," he went on, "but I've got to go through your things." He searched everything thoroughly, even trying to take my ballpoint pen apart. I told him he could keep that. He took all the written materials and put them on one side. "Oh no! What if he keeps them? I *knew* I should have read through them. Oh dear, I'll never remember everything." He spoke. "Suppose I won't let you take these . . .?" "I'll be very sad. The letters I received were a great help to me. So were the words I wrote down from my Bible." "Dear Lord, please make him change his mind . . ." At last he had finished his examination and was satisfied. I held my breath . . . he picked up the pile of notepaper and put it on top of the other things I could take. "Thank you, Lord." The only things he kept back were a couple of items of medicine and the torn-up letter, which seemed to embarrass him. I changed my clothes and packed up my box. There wasn't much to pack – just my remaining clothes and toilet articles, my written materials and a few oddments. There was my shell, still in the bottom of the box – how small it looked, but so pretty. I was glad it hadn't been lost. Was it really only three weeks ago that I had picked it up on the beach? What a lot had happened since then. Now it was going home with me, as a reminder of God's goodness in delivering me.

At about midday we set off for a walk to the shore. It was hot. I was told to wear my *tadjung* over my head and shoulders as a disguise and this made me even hotter. The trail took us through coconut and banana groves, past houses and across streams. At one point we lost the trail and had to make our way through a field of long coarse grass known as *cogon*. There were rocks hidden underneath it and I had to move forward carefully, to avoid twisting an ankle.

From a high point on a ridge we could see two speedboats, anchored some distance from the shore. They said, "That's your transport down there." They had already told me there was an "Americano" on board and I was sure it was Seymour. I wondered who else was there and who the speedboats belonged to. I had expected to go home the way I had come, by pumpboat.

When we got to the shore, there was a big crowd of people sitting around. I recognised several of the Tausug family from the first house. H–'s mother was there but there was no sign of Commander J–, or H–, or the negotiator. So we sat down and waited while people gathered around once more to have a look at me. We were probably there about half an hour before everyone else arrived, Commander J–, the *hadji*, H–, and his two brothers. Then I was told, "Now you can go home. Ask permission to go home." So I took my leave of the crowd in the proper Muslim fashion, saying, "I will now ask permission to go home."

We boarded the pumpboat and set off. It wasn't until we were in sight of the speedboats and I could see the guns and soldiers that I realised they were Philippine Constabulary boats. I had thought I would be going home quietly with H– and his family, the *hadji*, and Seymour. Then I realised how it had turned out.

I could see Seymour – he was waving to me – and

Ralph Jacobson, one of the SIL pilots, with camera poised. Now the Colonel was reaching down to haul me on board. I heard his words, "You're safe!" I was thankful, so thankful.

But I had really been safe all along . . . truly the Lord had done great things for me, and I was glad.

Epilogue

Many other people were glad too. I was amazed to find a big crowd waiting on the pier in Zamboanga City – Jo Ann, other missionary friends, Filipino friends and of course Sulaiman. How good it was to see them all again. They had prayed for my release and were now seeing the answer to their prayers.

Arriving at the SIL Centre at Nasuli was even more overwhelming. The excited crowd at the hangar reminded me of the Millers' arrival some five months earlier. Little had I realised then that the next person to be so eagerly awaited would be me. When I discovered that my SIL colleagues and Filipino friends had been praying for me day and night and thinking of every practical detail to pray about, I was very humbled. It certainly had been true that "there were many with me" (Psalm 55:18).

The Philippine authorities had successfully negotiated to secure my safe release and many Filipino friends of SIL had prayed, so it was appropriate that they should be honoured at a reception organised in Manila by Dr. Richard Pittman. It was a wonderful opportunity for us to thank both them and God for the happy outcome of their work and prayers. And I saw the beginning, then, of my opportunities to "declare the works of the Lord" (Psalm 118:17) as God had promised me.

Six weeks after my release, I returned home to England to begin my normal furlough, and be reunited with my family and friends who had wept and prayed over me. Once again I was amazed to learn of so many who had prayed, not only in England, but in all parts of the world. Many of you who have read this book were among them, and to you I express my heartfelt thanks for your vital help. Together we have seen the goodness of the Lord and together we can praise Him for the great things He has done in answer to prayer.